Level 3: 750 vocabulary words

The Courtesan Li Wa

李娃传

侯琨 改编

MP3 Download Online
www.sinolingua.com.cn

First Edition   2016

ISBN 978-7-5138-1102-6
Copyright 2016 by Sinolingua Co., Ltd
Published by Sinolingua Co., Ltd
24 Baiwanzhuang Road, Beijing 100037, China
Tel: (86) 10-68320585   68997826
Fax: (86) 10-68997826   68326333
http://www.sinolingua.com.cn
E-mail: hyjx@sinolingua.com.cn
Facebook: www.facebook.com/sinolingua
Printed by Beijing Jinghua Hucais Printing Co., Ltd

Printed in the People's Republic of China

编者的话

对于广大汉语学习者来说，要想快速提高汉语水平，扩大阅读量是很有必要的。"彩虹桥"汉语分级读物为汉语学习者提供了一系列有趣、有用的汉语阅读材料。本系列读物按照词汇量进行分级，力求用限定的词汇讲述精彩的故事。本套读物主要有以下特点：

一、分级精准，循序渐进。我们参考"新汉语水平考试（HSK）词汇表"（2012年修订版）、《汉语国际教育用音节汉字词汇等级划分（国家标准）》和《常用汉语1500高频词语表》等词汇分级标准，结合《欧洲语言教学与评估框架性共同标准》（CEFR），设计了一套适合汉语学习者的"彩虹桥"词汇分级标准。本系列读物分为7个级别（入门级*、1级、2级、3级、4级、5级、6级），供不同水平的汉语学习者选择，每个级别故事的生词数量不超过本级别对应词汇量的20%。随着级别的升高，故事的篇幅逐渐加长。本系列读物与HSK、CEFR的对应级别，各级词汇量以及每本书的字数详见下表。

---

* 入门级（Starter）在封底用S标识。

级别	入门级	1级	2级	3级	4级	5级	6级
对应级别	HSK1 CEFR A1	HSK1-2 CEFR A1-A2	HSK2-3 CEFR A2-B1	HSK3 CEFR A2-B1	HSK3-4 CEFR B1	HSK4 CEFR B1-B2	HSK5 CEFR B2-C1
词汇量	150	300	500	750	1 000	1 500	2 500
字数	1 000	2 500	5 000	7 500	10 000	15 000	25 000

二、**故事精彩，题材多样**。本套读物选材的标准就是"精彩"，所选的故事要么曲折离奇，要么感人至深，对读者构成奇妙的吸引力。选题广泛取材于中国的神话传说、民间故事、文学名著、名人传记和历史故事等，让汉语学习者在阅读中潜移默化地了解中国的文化和历史。

三、**结构合理，实用性强**。"彩虹桥"系列读物的每一本书中，除了中文故事正文之外，都配有主要人物的中英文介绍、生词英文注释及例句、故事正文的英文翻译、练习题和生词表，方便读者阅读和理解故事内容，提升汉语阅读能力。练习题主要采用客观题，题型多样，难度适中，并附有参考答案，既可供汉语教师在课堂上教学使用，又可供汉语学习者进行自我水平检测。

如果您对本系列读物有什么想法，比如推荐精彩故事、提出改进意见等，请发邮件到 liuxiaolin@sinolingua.com.cn，与我们交流探讨。也可以关注我们的微信公众号 CHQRainbowBridge，随时与我们交流互动。同时，微信公众号会不定期发布有关"彩虹桥"的出版信息，以及汉语阅读、中国文化小知识等。

韩　颖　刘小琳

Preface

For students who study Chinese as a foreign language, it's crucial for them to enlarge the scope of their reading to improve their comprehension skills. The "Rainbow Bridge" Graded Chinese Reader series is designed to provide a collection of interesting and useful Chinese reading materials. This series grades each volume by its vocabulary level and brings the learners into every scene through vivid storytelling. The series has the following features:

I. A gradual approach by grading the volumes based on vocabulary levels. We have consulted the New HSK Vocabulary (2012 Revised Edition), the *Graded Chinese Syllables, Characters and Words for the Application of Teaching Chinese to the Speakers of Other Languages (National Standard)* and the 1500 Commonly Used High Frequency Chinese Vocabulary, along with the Common European Framework of Reference for Languages (CEFR) to design the "Rainbow Bridge" vocabulary grading standard. The series is divided into seven levels (Starter*, Level 1, Level 2, Level 3, Level 4, Level 5 and Level 6) for students at different stages in their Chinese education to choose from. For each level, new words are no more than 20% of the vocabulary amount as specified in the corresponding HSK and CEFR levels.

---

* Represented by "S" on the back cover.

As the levels progress, the passage length will in turn increase. The following table indicates the corresponding "Rainbow Bridge" level, HSK and CEFR levels, the vocabulary amount, and number of characters.

Level	Starter	1	2	3	4	5	6
HSK/ CEFR Level	HSK1 CEFR A1	HSK1-2 CEFR A1-A2	HSK2-3 CEFR A2-B1	HSK3 CEFR A2-B1	HSK3-4 CEFR B1	HSK4 CEFR B1-B2	HSK5 CEFR B2-C1
Vocabulary	150	300	500	750	1,000	1,500	2,500
Characters	1,000	2,500	5,000	7,500	10,000	15,000	25,000

II. Intriguing stories on various themes. The series features engaging stories known for their twists and turns as well as deeply touching plots. The readers will find it a joyful experience to read the stories. The topics are selected from Chinese mythology, legends, folklore, literary classics, biographies of renowned people and historical tales. Such widely ranged topics would exert an invisible, yet formative, influence on readers' understanding of Chinese culture and history.

III. Reasonably structured and easy to use. For each volume of the "Rainbow Bridge" series, apart from a Chinese story, we also provide an introduction to the main characters in Chinese and English, new words with English explanations and sample sentences, and an English translation of the story, followed by comprehension exercises and a vocabulary list to help users read and understand the story and improve their Chinese reading skills. The exercises are mainly presented as objective questions that take on various forms with moderate difficulty. Moreover, keys to the exercises are also provided. The series can be used by teachers in class or by students for self-study.

If you have any questions, comments or suggestions about the series, please email us at liuxiaolin@sinolingua.com.cn. You can also exchange ideas with us via our WeChat account: CHQRainbowBridge. This account will provide updates on the series along with Chinese reading materials and cultural tips.

Han Ying and Liu Xiaolin

主要人物和地点
Main Characters and Places

高老爷 (Gāo lǎoye)：常州的大官，只有一个儿子。
Lord Gao: An official in Changzhou, who had only one son.

高公子 (Gāo gōngzǐ)：高老爷的儿子，书读得很好。
Lord Gao Junior: The son of Lord Gao, who excelled in his study.

李娃 (Lǐ Wá)：长安的妓女，非常漂亮。
Li Wa: A beautiful courtesan in Chang'an.

李娃的养母 (Lǐ Wá de yǎngmǔ)：十年前买了李娃，用李娃骗了很多钱。
Li Wa's adoptive mother: She bought Li Wa ten years ago, and earned a lot of money because of her.

常州 (Chángzhōu)：中国江苏省的一座城市。
Chang zhou: A city in Jiangsu Province of China.

长安 (Cháng'ān)：唐朝的都城，就是现在的陕西省西安市。
Chang'an: Capital city of the Tang Dynasty, which is present Xi'an in Shaanxi Province.

中文故事

李娃传

爱上美人

唐朝①的时候,常州有个大官②,姓高,常州人都叫他"高老爷"。高老爷是个很好的官,在常州住了很多年,为人们做过很多好事,这里的人都非常感谢他。

高老爷的家里只有一个儿子,人们都叫他"高公子"。高公子非常聪明,人长得也很好看,人们都喜欢他。高公子读书很用心,在学校考试的成绩总是第一名。当地人都说:"这个孩子现在就这么聪明,以后一定能当状元③的。"

高老爷和妻子听了这

① 唐朝 (Tángcháo) n. Tang Dynasty (618—907)

② 大官 (dà guān) n. high-ranking official e.g., 包公是中国古代一位了不起的大官,老百姓都很爱戴他。

③ 状元 (Zhuàngyuan) n. Number One Scholar in a nationwide imperial examination

话非常开心。高老爷常常得意地对别人说:"这孩子是我家的骄傲啊。他将来一定会成为一个了不起的人!"

这一年,高老爷50岁,高公子也19岁了。皇帝①在全国招考②状元,高老爷决定让儿子去长安参加考试。高老爷和妻子在儿子离家之前,准备好了一切。马车、高公子每天要读的书、高公子穿的衣

① 皇帝 (Huángdì) n. emperor

② 招考 (zhāokǎo) v. recruit through examination
e.g., 国家招考公务员,我参加了考试。

① 仆人 (púrén) *n.*
servant
e.g., 他小的时候家里很穷,妈妈给有钱人当仆人,供他上学。

② 两 (liǎng) *m.w.*
liang (a unit of weight, equal to 50 grams)
e.g., 我早上吃了三两包子,现在还觉得很饱呢。

③ 银子 (yínzi) *n.*
silver
e.g., 在纸币出现以前,人们使用金子和银子作为货币。

服,还有高公子路上要用的钱和在长安生活用的钱——那可是很多很多的钱啊,满满一大包呢!高老爷还让两个仆人①跟着高公子一起去长安,好在路上保护他。

高老爷对儿子说:"孩子,我和你母亲给你准备了3000两②银子③。这些钱够你在长安生活三年的了。如果今年考试结果不好，你就在长安住下，好好再读一年书。你还年轻，不用担心，等明年再考就是了。"

高公子虽然从来没有离开过家，但是他很自信①。他对父母说："你们放心吧，今年的状元一定是我的！"

高公子大约走了一个月，终于到了长安。高公子从没离开过家，更没有到过长安这么大的城市。在他眼里，长安到处都是好玩儿的东西。高公子和仆人们先找了家安静的宾馆②住下。这家宾馆里住的几乎都是外地来长安考

① 自信 (zìxìn) *adj.* confident
e.g., 自信的孩子在陌生人面前常常表现得更友好，也更乐于交流。

② 宾馆 (bīnguǎn) *n.* hotel
e.g., 这里是旅游区，宾馆很多，价钱都不贵。

① 骑 (qí) *v.* ride
e.g., 我的家离学校不远，我每天骑车10分钟就到学校了。

试的年轻人。这些年轻人一心想着考试，每天一大早就起来看书，几乎从不出门。

高公子一开始还看了几天书，可是一个月后，他就再也不想读书了。原来，高公子和宾馆里的年轻人研究了几次问题。他发现那些人的想法都不如他，他心里就有些得意了。他想："那些人每天都在读书，可是很多问题还是不会回答，还要请教我呢。我的学问比他们好太多了！"

这样一来，高公子决定先不看书了，还是每天出去逛逛吧。从那以后，他每天吃完早饭就骑①马出

门，东看看西看看，总要逛到天都黑了才回宾馆。

两个仆人看<u>高公子</u>这样，就说了他几次，可他一点儿也听不进去。仆人们多说他几句，他就会生气。后来，仆人们也不敢再说他了。

一天，<u>高公子</u>骑马经过一条大路，路口有个大<u>院子</u>①。<u>高公子</u>经过院子的

① 院子 (yuànzi) n. courtyard
e.g., 奶奶家有个大院子，院子里种着玉兰树。

① 侍女 (shìnǚ) *n.* maidservant
e.g., 公主的侍女们都长得非常漂亮。

② 回 (huí) *v.* return
e.g., 听到有人叫我的名字，我回过头去看了看。

时候，大门正好打开了。门里走出来一个小侍女①，后面跟着一个20岁左右的姑娘。这个姑娘太漂亮了，她不仅长得漂亮，穿得也很好看。这样好看的姑娘，高公子从来都没见过。他拉住了马，一动不动地在那里看着这个姑娘，看了很长时间。这个姑娘感觉有人在看她，就回②过头来。她也看到了高公子。

春风中，两个年轻人就这么对面站着，一动不动。高公子觉得自己好像已经和这个姑娘认识很多年了。一会儿，姑娘的脸先红了，她不好意思地回身进了大门。高公子也被姑娘看得脸上发烧，连耳朵都红了。他的心跳个不停，一心想知道这个姑娘是谁。

高公子不敢上前去叫门，但又不想就这样离开。于是①，他就去问邻居，那个姑娘到底是谁。邻居告诉他："那个漂亮姑娘是妓女②李娃，想和她交往的男人很多。你如果没有100两银子送给李娃的养母③，那个老太太④就不会让李娃和你见面。"

① 于是 (yúshì) conj. then
e.g., 我们赶到火车站的时候车已经开走了，于是，我们只能改坐下一趟火车。

② 妓女 (jìnǚ) n. courtesan
e.g., 夜幕降临的时候，打扮得花枝招展的妓女，三三两两地出现在昏暗的街道上。

③ 养母 (yǎngmǔ) n. adoptive mother
e.g., 这个孩子的养母很善良，对他很好。

④ 老太太 (lǎotàitai) n. old lady
e.g., 这个老太太对人很和气。

① 敲 (qiāo) v. knock
e.g., 我在大门上轻轻敲了两下，一个老人来给我开了门。

第二天，高公子穿上最好的衣服，拿了300两银子，来到李娃家门口。他敲①了敲门，过了一会儿，一个小侍女来开了门。高公子一看，这正是昨天和李娃一起站在门口的那个小侍女。小侍女也认出了高公子，回头对着房间里的李娃大声说："姐姐快出来啊，昨天那个骑马的人又来了！"

李娃在东边的房间里听到了侍女的话，心里非常高兴，连忙大声回答："让他先等等，我打扮好就来见他。"

一听李娃愿意见自己，高公子心里很高兴。这时候，一个老太太从南边的

房子里走出来,她说自己是李娃的养母,请高公子进去坐。

　　高公子和老太太走进房间。这房间里面可真大啊,家具也都不便宜。高公子想:"看来,不送给老太太一些银子,她是不会让我见李娃的。"于是,他坐下后,马上拿出150两银子放在桌子上。老太太一看到这么多钱,就笑着

① 您 (nín) *pron.* you, a polite form of 你 e.g., 这个年轻人很有礼貌，和老人说话时用"您"，不用"你"。

说："我有个女儿，从小就活泼可爱。她喜欢唱歌跳舞，也喜欢和您①这样有文化的年轻人交朋友。我这就让她来和您见面。请您先坐一会儿。"

老太太出去了一会儿，李娃就进来了。李娃真的非常漂亮，她的眼睛大大的，头发又长又黑，小手雪白；她穿着好看的红衣服，走起路来美极了。高

公子吃惊地站了起来,眼睛看着李娃,不知道该说什么才好。

　　侍女送来茶水,李娃客气地请高公子喝茶,还开心①地和高公子说说笑笑。在高公子眼里,李娃的笑特别美,说话的声音特别美,动作也特别美。高公子以前②想都没有想过,世界上还有这样的美人。

　　中午,侍女送来饭菜和酒,李娃和高公子一边吃饭一边聊天。高公子红着脸对李娃说:"自从③昨天见到你,我回去就再也吃不下饭了,一个晚上我怎么也睡不着。我的心里一直想着你。"李娃听了这话也害羞地低下了头,小声

① 开心 (kāixīn) adj.
happy
e.g., 我们开心地走进了公园。

② 以前 (yǐqián) n.
before
e.g., 回美国以前,我要去北京玩几天。

③ 自从 (zìcóng) prep.
from, since
e.g., 自从开学以后,我就没有见过她。

① 人生 (rénshēng) *n.*
life
e.g., 他今年结婚了，完成了一件人生大事。

② 干涉 (gānshèn) *v.*
meddle, intervene
e.g., 这是我的事，请你不要干涉。

说："我心里也是一样的。"高公子非常高兴，他觉得和李娃在一起的感觉太幸福了。两个人在一起有说不完的话。就这样，他们两个人一直聊到了吃晚饭的时候。

这时，老太太走进客厅，问高公子住得远不远。高公子连忙说："我住得很远，天已经黑了，这时候回去路上不安全。"说着，高公子又拿出100两银子放在了桌子上。

老太太拿了钱，笑着说："爱情是人生①最美好的事。年轻人的爱情，是父母都不能干涉②的。我希望我的女儿能找到对她好的男朋友。"高公子一听这话，马上把身上带的钱都拿出来放在了桌子上。他对老太太说："请让我和您的女儿交朋友，我会对她好的。"老太太拿了钱，满意地点点头走了。

第二天早上，高公子回到宾馆，让两个仆人把他的东西全都送到李娃家里。高公子告诉仆人们："以后①我们三个人要住在

① 以后 (yǐhòu) n. later
e.g., 长大以后，他成了一名医生。

<u>李娃</u>家，那里更安静，我要在那里读书。"从那以后，<u>高公子</u>和两个仆人就都在李家住下了。

两个仆人很担心<u>高公子</u>，怕他和妓女<u>李娃</u>学坏了，变成只想着玩儿、不做正事的人。如果是这样，那可怎么好啊？<u>高老爷</u>如果知道了，一定要气死了！

一天，两个仆人看房间里没别人，就对<u>高公子</u>说："考试时间快到了，公子你要早做准备啊。你现在每天不读书怎么行啊？如果老爷知道了……""我知道了，知道了。不要说了！"<u>高公子</u>才没心情听仆人们说话呢，他又跑到房子外面和<u>李娃</u>唱歌去了。

李娃和高公子的感情越来越好，他们每天在一起唱歌、说笑，一起出门去玩儿。这样的日子过得虽然快乐，可是花的钱却很多。高公子从家里带来的钱很快就花完了。他只好卖掉了马和车子，后来连两个仆人都卖掉了。过了一年，高公子再也拿不出钱了。慢慢地，老太太对他的态度①越来越不好。

① 态度 (tàidù) *n.* manner, bearing
e.g., 这个服务员对待客人的态度非常好。

① 主意 (zhǔyi) *n.*
idea
e.g., 这个事情大家不要着急，一起想想，一定能想出个好主意。

② 租 (zū) *v.* rent
e.g., 周末我租了辆越野车，带上父母和宠物狗一起去郊外玩儿了一天。

③ 花园 (huāyuán) *n.*
garden
e.g., 这个花园非常大，里面种了几十种花。

④ 养女 (yǎngnǚ) *n.*
adoptive daughter
e.g., 这对夫妇对他们的养女很好。

美人离去

有一天，李娃对高公子说："最近天气很凉快，我想去有山有水的地方玩儿几天，你说好吗？"高公子不知道李娃和她的养母打了坏主意①，马上就同意了。高公子租②了一辆马车，和李娃一起离开了长安。他们找了个有山有水的地方住下，玩儿了两天，到第三天下午才回长安。

马车经过一个花园③的时候，李娃忽然对高公子说："我姐姐的家就在这里，我们去看看她吧。"高公子问李娃："我怎么从来没听你说过，你还有个姐姐啊？"

李娃说："她和我一样，

也是养女①,已经结婚很多年了。她很少去看养母的。"

他们来到花园门口,敲了敲门。一个矮个子侍女来开门,问他们是谁。李娃说:"我是李娃,来看姐姐。"

等了一会儿,一个30多岁的女人和矮个子侍女一起来到门口。那个女人一看到李娃就笑着拉住她说:"妹妹,你怎么来了?

养母身体还好吗？"李娃笑着和她问好，然后介绍高公子和她认识。

　　姐姐笑着请他们两个人到花园里参观。花园很大，里面开了很多很美的花。花园中间还放着一张大桌子。三个人参观过花园，就一起坐在桌子旁边休息、聊天。矮个子侍女送来了很多水果。高公子一边吃水果，一边小声问李娃："这是姐姐的家吗？这花园可真大啊！"李娃好像没听见，笑着对高公子说："这茶可好喝了，你快喝喝看。"

　　过了一会儿，李娃说要到门口的车里去拿个东西给姐姐看，让高公子和姐姐等等她。高公子要跟她一起去。李娃说："不用了，我让侍女和我去吧。女人用的东西，你不要看。"高公子只好坐下，继续喝茶。

　　过了一会儿，矮个子侍女一个人回来了，手里还拿着一封①信。李娃却没有回来。高公子很担心，连忙②问出了什么事。矮个子侍女说："刚才门口来了一个小孩儿，好像认识李娃，他给了她这封信。李娃读了信，让我把信给高公子送来，自己就上车走了。"

　　高公子赶紧③拿过信来看。信是一家医馆④里的大夫写的，信上说李娃的

① 封 (fēng) m.w. (for sth. enveloped)
e.g., 今天我收到一封信。

② 连忙 (liánmáng) adv. immediately
e.g., 听到上课铃声，我连忙往教室跑去。

③ 赶紧 (gǎnjǐn) adv. hurriedly, without delay
e.g., 天气预报说傍晚有大雨，妈妈让我放学后赶紧回家，别在路上耽搁。

④ 医馆 (yīguǎn) n. hospital (in ancient times)
e.g., 城里一共有四家医馆，这一家离我住的地方最近。

① 急 (jí) *adj.*
irritated, anxious
e.g., 这个小男孩儿找不着妈妈了，急得大哭起来。

养母病得很重，快要死了，让李娃快去医馆见她。高公子一下子急①了，对着李娃的姐姐激动地大叫起来："这么重要的事，她怎么一个人就去了，怎么不和我一起去呢？"

一直坐在旁边的姐姐拿过信来看了看，也说："这个李娃，怎么不说一声就跑了。不过，你也不要太生气了。李娃一定是担心母亲，一下子不知道该怎么办。我这就让侍女出门给你找个车来，你也快去医馆找她吧。"

高公子这时候心里又生气又担心，可是也没有办法，只好等侍女帮他找马车来。过了很长时间，马车终于到了大门口。高公子坐车赶到了信里说的那家医馆。医馆里的人却告诉他，今天没有来过什么李娃母女。

高公子怀疑是医馆的地址写错了，就让马车送他回李娃家。高公子在路上想："他们可能已经先回家了。或者是李娃的养母突然死了，他们都去棺材铺①了？要不就是他们去了

① 棺材铺
(guāncaipù) *n.*
coffin shop
e.g., 棺材铺老板是个好心的人。

别的医馆……"

到了吃晚饭的时候，马车终于来到李娃家。走进大门一看，高公子吃惊得一句话也说不出来了。他发现，每个房间都是黑的，一个人都没有。他叫了几声，也没有人回答。他走进每个房间，发现房间里的家具也都不见了。

高公子不知道发生了什么事，半天说不出话来。

他站在大门口想了半天，不敢相信那么爱他的<u>李娃</u>会这样离开他。

他不相信，他说什么也不相信。他相信<u>李娃</u>是爱他的，一定是爱他的。

他要找她问个明白。

门口的马车已经离开了。他一个人走了很长时间的路，终于找到了下午去过的那个花园门口。他又累又气，用了很大的力气去敲那厚厚的大门。可是，天那么晚了，大家都睡觉了，哪儿还会有人来给他开门呢？他坐在花园门口的地上哭了起来。他又渴又饿，哭着哭着就睡着了。

等他<u>醒</u>①过来，已经是

---

① 醒 (xǐng) v.
wake up
e.g., 儿子昨天晚上睡得很晚，今天上午一直在睡觉，到吃午饭的时候才醒来。

第二天早上了。他又用力地敲门。不一会儿,一个老仆人来开门,问他要干什么。他说:"我要找<u>李娃</u>。不,我要找<u>李娃</u>的姐姐。这是她的家吧?"

老仆人用怀疑的眼光看着他说:"年轻人,你找错地方了吧?这是张家花园啊!张家人都不住在<u>长</u>

安。他们家里只有一位90岁的老太太，再没有别的女人了。我是这家的仆人，在这里看花园20年了，从来没听说过什么李娃和她的姐姐啊！"高公子不相信，说："不对！我昨天下午还来过这个花园。是一个矮个子侍女开的门。"

老仆人想了想说："啊，我知道了。因为张家人很少来花园，所以这个花园常常租出去。前天是有个矮个子侍女来租花园。她说是她的女主人一家要来这里玩两天。可是他们昨天吃晚饭的时候就走了呀。花园里现在没有人，不信你进去找找看。"高公子在花园里找了又找……

最后，他坐在花园中间的桌子旁大哭起来。

过了一会儿，<u>高公子</u>安静了下来，喝了些老仆人拿给他的茶水。然后，<u>高公子</u>把这一年来的生活和昨天发生的事都讲给这位老仆人听了。

老仆人听完，看着他说："年轻人，听了你说的

这些事，我看啊，你大概是被妓女骗①了。你这样的外地年轻人，大多是带了不少钱来长安考试的，在长安没什么朋友，那些坏人就是看中了这一点。发生这样的事情也真是不幸②。你还是快点儿想办法联系父母，让他们早点接③你回家吧。"

生不如死

高公子后悔④极了。他没有地方去，也没有认识的人，他觉得自己对不起父母，没有脸回家。他对李娃母女⑤很生气，但他更生自己的气。他走啊走啊，不知什么时候又走到了李娃家门口。他就这么呆⑥呆地坐在地上，不吃不喝，

① 骗 (piàn) v. deceive
e.g., 现在社会上有一些坏人，专门骗老人钱财。

② 不幸 (búxìng) adj. unfortunate
e.g., 幸福的婚姻是一样的，不幸的婚姻各有各的不幸。

③ 接 (jiē) v. pick up
e.g., 我每天一下班就要去幼儿园接孩子。

④ 后悔 (hòuhuǐ) v. regret, be remorseful
e.g., 大发脾气之后，这位母亲感到非常后悔。

⑤ 母女 (mǔnǚ) n. mother and daughter
e.g., 这对母女的感情很好。

⑥ 呆 (dāi) adv. in a daze
e.g., 她呆呆地看着我，一句话也不说。

① 同情 (tóngqíng) v. sympathize
e.g., 老人无儿无女，村里的人都很同情他。

② 难过 (nánguò) adj. sad, sorrowful
e.g., 小猫不见了，我很难过。

觉得自己生不如死。

邻居们听说了他的事，都很同情①他，有几个人还拿来饭菜给他吃，让他住在自己家的大门口。不管怎么说，睡在邻居家的大门口总比睡在路边要好些。高公子心里非常难过②，觉得自己连狗都不如。

很快，高公子得了很重的病，几乎要死了。于是，邻居们把他送到了棺材铺里。大家虽然都同情他，可是也没有办法。

棺材铺里的人都很好心，他们每天拿鸡蛋汤①给他喝，希望他能好起来。一个月后，高公子的病好多了，能自己站起来了。他没地方可以去，于是就留在棺材铺帮忙。这一干就是三年。

高公子字写得很好，还很会唱歌。这可帮了老板②大忙。原来，唐朝的时候，人们家里有人去世③，都要请棺材铺的人来唱歌。歌里唱的都是死去的人以前做过的好事。

① 汤 (tāng) n. soup
e.g., 南方人习惯先喝汤后吃饭，北方人则正好相反。

② 老板 (lǎobǎn) n. shop owner
e.g., 我们老板人不错。

③ 去世 (qùshì) v. pass away
e.g., 他的老师去世了，他很难过。

① 流泪 (liú lèi) v.
weep
e.g., 这是一部让人看了流泪的电影。

② 市场 (shìchǎng) n.
market
e.g., 这是城里最大的市场。

③ 举行 (jǔxíng) v.
hold, host
e.g., 我们秋天举行婚礼，到时候你一定要来啊。

④ 当地 (dāngdì) n.
locality
e.g., 这个小饭馆的菜很好吃，当地的人都知道。

死去的人的亲人朋友听到这样的歌，都会感动得流泪①，还会给棺材铺的人很多钱。因此，那些唱歌唱得好的人很受欢迎。

长安城里，每三年都会在最大的市场②里举行③一次比赛，看哪家棺材铺的人唱的歌最好。高公子读过很多书，很会写歌。他写的歌非常有感情，唱出来最能感动人。这一年，唱歌比赛的时间又到了，棺材铺老板就让高公子去比赛。

比赛要进行三天，很多人都来听唱歌。不仅长安当地④的人来听，连到长安来玩儿的外地人也都来听。在听歌的人里，有

一个是高公子认识的——他常州家中的一个老仆人。这个老仆人在高老爷家工作了30年,是看着高公子长①大的。老仆人站在很远的地方看着这个正在唱歌的年轻人,说什么也不敢相信自己的眼睛。

　　那个年轻人就是高公子啊!可是,他又怀疑是

① 长 (zhǎng) v. grow e.g., 他长得高高的、瘦瘦的。

自己看错了。高公子怎么会在这里唱歌呢？老仆人向旁边的人打听这个唱歌的年轻人是哪儿的人。人家告诉他，这是个常州人，被妓女骗光了钱，也不敢回家见父母，就留在这里了。

老仆人想："那就错不了了，这个年轻人一定是我家高公子。我要快去告诉我家老爷才行。"那么，这个老仆人怎么会来长安呢？原来，他是和高老爷一起到长安办事情的。高老爷工作的时候，老仆人就出门逛逛，走着走着就到了这个大市场。

老仆人一路小跑着回到高老爷住的宾馆。一进门，老仆人就哭着对高老爷说，他看见高公子了。高老爷听了老仆人的话，吃惊地说："什么？你真的看到我的儿子了？他在哪里？"

老仆人说了大市场里唱歌比赛的事，还说了李娃和高公子的事……高老爷听了，一点儿也不信，

① 消息 (xiāoxi) n.
news
e.g., 战争开始后，家里人就再也没有他的一点儿消息了。

② 转身 (zhuǎnshēn)
v. turn around
e.g., 她听到有人喊她的名字，转身一看，原来是张老师。

他说："你一定是看错了。我的儿子是个好孩子，心里只想着读书。他怎么会爱上妓女呢？那年他带着3000两银子和仆人离开家，就再没有消息① 了。我想他一定是在路上被坏人杀了。他怎么会给棺材铺唱歌呢？一定是长得像他的人吧！"

　　老仆人哭着让高老爷一定去看看。高老爷只好坐上马车，跟老仆人一起到了市场。这时，已经过了中午，看唱歌的人都回家了。高公子和几个年轻人正在市场打扫。老仆人走过去一把拉住高公子的衣服。高公子抬头一看，是自家的老仆人，转身② 就想

跑。老仆人两手拉住他,哭着叫道:"公子,你去哪儿啊?你父亲来了!你还要去哪儿啊……"

高公子觉得没脸见父亲,可是又被老仆人哭得心软①了。最后,他被老仆人拉到了马车旁。高老爷一直坐在车上远远地看着这一切。高公子上了车,心里非常害怕。他不敢看父亲,高老爷也冷着脸不

① 心软 (xīnruǎn) adj. tender-hearted
e.g., 妈妈是个心软的人,看见别人有难处总要出钱出力帮一把。

① 举起 (jǔqǐ) v.
lift, raise
e.g., 他把儿子高高地举起，儿子高兴得哈哈大笑。

② 鞭子 (biānzi) n.
whip
e.g., 父亲非常生气，将鞭子狠狠地打在儿子身上。

③ 浑身 (húnshēn) n.
all over the body
e.g., 在雨天里走了大半天山路的旅行者们，浑身都是泥巴。

④ 血 (xiě) n. blood
e.g., 车祸现场满地是血，看着就让人害怕。

⑤ 品行 (pǐnxíng) n.
moral conduct
e.g., 评价一个学生的时候，我们不应该只看他的成绩，更要看他的品行。

看他。高老爷对老仆人说了声"去城外"，就再也不说话了。

到了城外，高老爷让仆人在车旁等着，自己拉着儿子下了车。到了一个没人的地方，高老爷举起①鞭子②就打，打得高公子浑身③是血④。高老爷一边打一边骂，打到后来，高公子已经不能动了。

高老爷哭着对高公子说："四年前，你离开家后就没了消息，我和你母亲都以为你是在路上被坏人杀了，难过得要死。哪知道，你原来是在长安和妓女……我们家怎么会生出你这样坏品行⑤的儿子！我今天要打死你，就当我

没生过你。我再不是你的父亲,你也不再是我的儿子。"说完,<u>高老爷</u>就一个人离开了。

浑身是血、痛得要死的<u>高公子</u>呆呆地躺① 在地上。他多希望自己现在已经死了啊!他觉得对不起父母。他觉得没脸再活下去了。他不想再去唱歌了。他真想就这样死了算了。

① 躺 (tǎng) v. lie
e.g., 我刚躺下,门铃就响了。

① 游逛 (yóuguàng) v. stroll about, wander e.g., 他大学毕业后无心工作，一天到晚四处游逛。

再见美人

从那天起，高公子就在长安城里四处游逛①、要饭。他活着就跟死了一样。

很快，冬天到了。在一个大雪天的早上，高公子又冷又饿，站在大雪地里要饭。当他走到一条小路上的时候，看到有一个院子的大门正开着

半边。他就来到门前坐下，大声要饭："饿死我了！饿死我了！可怜①可怜我吧！给我点儿饭吃吧！"他的声音那么可怜，让人听了就想哭。高公子不知道这大门里住的就是李娃。

这时，李娃在自己的房间里听到了高公子的声音。她非常吃惊，对侍女说："这一定是高公子！我听出他的声音了。"说完她就跑了出来。

高公子已经不像人样了，他变得很瘦②，身上的衣服很少。看见李娃，他一句话没说就晕③了过去。李娃上前一把抱住他，让侍女帮着扶他回到自己房间。李娃让高公子躺在自

① 可怜 (kělián) v. have pity on, show mercy on
e.g., 人们可怜这个卖菜的人身体不好，买菜的时候总会多给他些钱。

② 瘦 (shòu) adj. thin
e.g., 他长得又高又瘦。

③ 晕 (yūn) adj. dizzy, fainted
e.g., 天太热了，出来游玩的孩子有好几个都晕倒了。

④ 床 (chuáng) n. bed
e.g., 酒店的房间很大，床也很软。

己的床①上，又让侍女拿热汤来给他喝。

李娃一边用热水给高公子洗身体，一边哭着说："你变成今天这样，都是因为我啊！"李娃的养母听见李娃房间里有声音，就跑过来看发生了什么事。一看是高公子，她马上对侍女说："快把这个要饭的赶走！为什么要让他进门？"

李娃非常生气，对养母说："不行！他是好人家的儿子，当年带着那么多钱来到我家，不到一年，钱就花光了。我们想办法赶走了他，他不能回家，也没有地方去。我们以前的邻居都知道他是因为我李娃才变成这样的。他的父亲母亲家有很多朋友在长安。如果有一天他们知道了高公子的事，要来找我们，那时候你跑得了吗？"

坏心的养母一听这话害怕了。李娃看着养母的眼睛说："我被卖给您做女儿已经十年了。我为您骗来的钱已经有几万两了。

现在您60岁了,为了您以后的生活,我就再给您10000两银子。从现在开始,我要离开您,和<u>高公子</u>一起生活。如果您不同意,那以后我就不再把您当我的养母了。"

老太太没有别的办法，只好拿了钱，让李娃离开了。李娃离开时手里还有1000两银子。她想："用这些钱，我和高公子可以生活很长时间了。"李娃到城外租了一个小院子，和高公子一起住下。李娃每天给高公子做饭，给他请大夫看病。过了几个月，高公子的身体好多了，李娃又带他去买了很多书回来。

高公子身体完全好了以后，李娃就叫他每天学习，准备来年的状元考试。这一次，高公子一心学习，每天除了吃饭睡觉，眼睛都不离开书。晚上，李娃常常坐在高公子身旁看他

① 派 (pài) v.
send, dispatch
e.g., 领导派我们两个人去买中秋联欢会上要用的东西。

② 成都 (Chéngdū) n.
Chengdu, capital city of Sichuan Province

学习。

　　第二年考试的时候,高公子真的中了状元。皇帝派①他去成都②做地方官。高公子要离开长安的时候,李娃对他说:"现在你终于像你父母希望的那样成了状元,我已经对得起你了。我该走了。虽然我很爱你,

可是我以前是妓女，你是好人家的儿子，现在又是地方官，我们不能结婚。你应该找一个有钱的大小姐结婚。现在，我要回到养母那里去了。她老了，不能一个人生活。"

　　高公子说什么也不同意，哭着说："你如果离开我，我马上去死。没有你，我不能活下去……"李娃没办法，只好和高公子说好，送他到成都后，她再离开。

① 团圆 (tuányuán) v. have a reunion
e.g., 春节是中国人全家团圆的日子。

大团圆 ①

高公子和李娃走了20多天，路上忽然在一家宾馆里遇到了高老爷的老仆人。这是怎么回事？原来，高老爷有工作上的事经过这里，也住在这家宾馆。父子二人住进了同一家宾馆，这还真是让人想不到呢！

高公子去找父亲认错，

高老爷一看儿子还活着，眼泪就流了下来。父子二人抱着哭了很长时间，终于和好①了。高老爷关心地问儿子这两年是怎么生活的。高公子全告诉了父亲，也说了李娃要离开的事。

　　高公子说完，高老爷低头想了很长时间，然后说："不能这样。要不是李娃帮你，你怎么可能有机会重新②做人呢？要不是李娃，我们高家现在就真的没有你这个儿子了，你也当不了状元。这件事，你们俩就听我安排吧。"

　　第二天早上，高老爷先叫了马车送高公子去成都。第三天，他让仆人租了一个院子，安排李娃住

① 和好 (héhǎo) v. become reconciled
e.g., 他们俩争吵之后很快就和好了。

② 重新 (chóngxīn) adv. anew, again
e.g., 我的书不见了，我只好重新买一本。

① 提亲 (tíqīn) v.
bring up a proposal of marriage on behalf of a boy's or girl's family
e.g., 过去的年轻人有了喜欢的人，要让父母代表自己去对方家提亲。

② 儿媳 (érxí) n.
daughter-in-law
e.g., 李老太太的儿媳是个又能干又孝顺的人。

下。第四天，高老爷让人到李娃那里提亲①。他准备让李娃和高公子结婚。

李娃没想到高老爷会让他们结婚，她感动得哭了。李娃是个好妻子，也是个好儿媳②。她结婚后一直都对高公子的父母非常好。高老爷和妻子也很喜欢李娃。从那以后，高公子一家过着幸福的生活。他们生了四个儿子，儿子

们过得也都很好。

　　许多年过去了，在<u>长安</u>还有很多老人会讲<u>李娃</u>的故事。因为<u>李娃</u>对爱情<u>勇敢</u>①地付出，不要求<u>回报</u>②，所以人们都很喜欢听她的故事。

---

① 勇敢 (yǒnggǎn) *adj.* brave, audacious
e.g., 他勇敢地从大火里救出了一个孩子。

② 回报 (huíbào) *v.* reward
e.g., 做好事不应该求回报。

English Version

The Courtesan Li Wa

Falling in Love with a Beauty

In the Tang Dynasty, there was a high-ranking official in Changzhou whose family name was Gao. The local residents called him Lord Gao. Lord Gao had resided here for many years and did a lot of good things for the people, so the locals loved him deeply.

Lord Gao had only one son, Lord Gao Junior, as he was called. He was very smart and good-looking, and the people were fond of him. He worked very hard at school and was always ranked at the top of the school tests. Local people said, "This child is so intelligent at an early age; he will surely become the Number One Scholar in the imperial examination one day."

Lord Gao and his wife were very delighted to hear that. Lord Gao often said to others with satisfaction, "Our family takes great pride in this child, and he will surely become someone in the future."

When Lord Gao was 50 years old, his son turned 19. In that year the imperial civil examination would be held nationwide. Lord Gao decided to send his son to take the test in the capital city, Chang'an. Before his son left home, Lord Gao and his wife

prepared what he needed, including a carriage, the books he would read every day, his clothes, traveling money and living expenses in Chang'an. They wanted to give him enough money, so they filled a big bag. Lord Gao asked two servants to go together with his son to Chang'an to protect him on the way.

Lord Gao told his son, "Dear son, your mother and I have prepared 3,000 taels of silver, which will be enough for you to live in Chang'an for three years. If you fail this year, you shall stay in Chang'an and study hard for another year. Don't worry about the test results. You are still young, and there will be another opportunity next year."

Although Gao had never been away from home, he had full confidence in himself. He told his parents, "Rest assured, I will be the Number One Scholar this year."

One month later, Gao arrived in Chang'an. He had never been to such a big city. In his eyes, interesting things abounded in Chang'an. Gao and his servants settled into a quiet hotel, in which nearly all the guests were young examinees from other places. These young people devoted themselves to the preparation of the examination: they got up early in the morning to read and hardly stepped out of the hotel.

Gao started to read books after he settled in. After one month, however, he was no longer willing to read books because he found the people in the hotel were less competent than him after several discussions. He began to feel arrogant and thought, "Although they study every day, they have to turn to me for many answers. I am far better than them."

Thus Gao decided to go sightseeing every day instead of reading. Each day after breakfast, he would ride a horse and wander in the city until dark.

The two servants alerted him several times, but he wouldn't accept what they said. When the servants kept reminding him, he would become angry. Afterwards, the servants dared not remind him anymore.

One day, Gao rode a horse across an avenue that had a big yard near the intersection. Its door happened to be open. A young maid came out followed by a girl in her twenties. This girl looked very pretty and was elegantly dressed. Gao had never seen such a beauty in his life. He pulled the horse and remained still, with his eyes fixed on the girl for a long time. The girl felt the gaze, turned around and noticed Gao.

The two stood face to face in the gentle spring breeze, motionless. Gao felt as though they had known each other for many years. After a while, the girl blushed and went back to the gate with hesitation. Gao also felt a fever in his face with his ears turning red as the girl gazed at him. His heart beat incessantly and he was eager to know who this girl was.

Although Gao dared not knock at the door, he was reluctant to leave. Instead, he went to ask her neighbor who that girl was. The neighbor told him, "That beautiful girl is Li Wa, a courtesan. Many people want to be her boyfriend. If you don't give her adoptive mother 100 taels of silver, she won't allow her daughter to meet you."

The next day, Gao wore his best clothes, took 300 taels of silver and came to Li Wa's house. He knocked at the door and soon a maid opened the door. Gao found that she was the maid standing with Li Wa at the gate yesterday. The maid also recognized Gao, then turned around and shouted to Li Wa in the room, "Come out, sister! The rider you saw yesterday came back!"

Li Wa stayed in the east room. After hearing what her servant said, she felt very delighted and answered loudly at once, "Have him wait a moment. After I get dressed, I will meet him."

Knowing Li Wa was ready to meet him, Gao was overjoyed. At this moment, an old lady walked out of the room in the south. She told him she was Li Wa's adoptive mother and then invited Gao into her room.

Gao walked inside the room with the old lady. He found this room was spaciously equipped with expensive furniture. Gao thought, "It seems that if I don't give her some money, she won't allow me to meet Li Wa." So immediately after sitting down, Gao took out 150 taels of silver and put it on the table. At the sight of so much money, the old lady said with a smile, "I have a daughter, and she has always been cute and cheerful. She likes singing and dancing and is also willing to make friends with an educated young man like you. I will ask her to meet you now. Please wait here."

Shortly after the old lady went out, Li Wa came in. She was really beautiful. She had big eyes, long, black hair and small, white hands. She was in red and walked gracefully. Gao stood up in shock, gazed at Li Wa and didn't know what to say.

The servant brought tea and Li Wa invited Gao to drink. Li Wa kept talking happily with Gao. In Gao's eyes, Li Wa smiled beautifully, moved elegantly and spoke with a sweet voice. Gao had never dreamed of such a beauty in the world.

At noon, the servant brought the meal and wine, and they ate their meal while chatting. Gao, with a red face, said to Li Wa,

"I didn't want to have meals anymore after I saw you yesterday. I couldn't fall asleep last night and kept missing you." Hearing this, Li Wa lowered her head with embarrassment and said in a low voice, "Me, too." Gao was extremely happy, and he felt that being together with Li Wa was a great joy. They talked on and on until it was dinner time.

At this moment, the old lady entered the living room and asked whether he lived far or not. Gao said immediately, "I live far away from here. It's getting dark now, and it's not safe to be back too late." With these words, he took out another 100 taels of silver and put them on the table.

The old lady held the money and said with a smile, "Love is the happiest thing in life. Parents cannot meddle in the love between a boy and a girl. I hope my daughter can find a boy who is kind to her." Hearing this, Gao took out all his money, put them on the table and said to her, "Please allow me to be your girl's boyfriend and I will treat her kindly." The old lady took the money, nodded her head with satisfaction and went away.

The next morning, Gao came back to the hotel and asked the two servants to take all his belongings to Li Wa's family. He told them, "We will live in Li Wa's house. Her house is quieter, so I can concentrate on my study there." Since then, Gao and his two servants settled in the Li's.

The two servants were worried about Gao and were afraid that he would indulge in playing with Li Wa and forget all about his study. What should they do then? If Lord Gao knew this, he would be furious.

Then one day when there was no other people in Gao's room, the two servants said to him, "The examination is approaching.

You should prepare for it as early as possible. How will you take the test if you don't read every day? If Lord Gao knew…." "I know, I know. Don't say that again." Gao was in no mood listening to what the servants had to say, and he ran outside and sang together with Li Wa again.

Li Wa and Gao were getting along better and better with each other. Every day they sang, talked, laughed and went out for fun. Although they enjoyed themselves every day, they spent a huge sum of money. Gao spent all the money he brought from his home, so later he had to sell his horse, his carriage and even his two servants. One year passed by and Gao had no money left. Gradually, the old lady became more and more dissatisfied with him.

The Beauty Left

One day Li Wa said to Gao, "It's been cool recently. Shall we go sightseeing in the mountainous area surrounded by water?" Gao agreed immediately, not knowing that Li Wa and her adoptive mother harbored an evil idea. He rented a carriage and left Chang'an with Li Wa. They settled in a mountainous area surrounded by water, played together for two days and headed back to Chang'an on the afternoon of the third day.

When their carriage passed by a garden right here, Li Wa suddenly said to Gao, "My sister lives right here. Let's go and visit her." Gao asked, "Why didn't you mention before that you had a sister?"

Li Wa said, "She is an adopted daughter like me. She has been married for many years, but seldom visited our mother."

They knocked at the gate of the garden. A short maidservant

opened the gate and asked who they were. Li Wa said, "I am Li Wa, and I come to see my sister."

After a while, a lady around 30 came to the gate accompanied by the short maidservant. At the sight of Li Wa, she held her hands and said with a smile, "Sister, what brings you here? How is our mother?" Li Wa smiled and greeted her, then introduced Gao to her.

Li Wa's sister invited them to her garden, in which there were a variety of flowers. In the middle of the garden there stood a big table. After visiting the garden, they sat beside the table for a rest and chat. The servant brought them many fruits. While Gao was eating the fruit, he asked Li Wa in a low voice, "Is this your sister's house? Her garden is so big!" Li Wa seemed to have heard nothing, and said with a smile to Gao, "This tea tastes so good. Want to try it?"

A moment later, Li Wa said she would take something from the carriage at the gate and show it to her sister. She asked Gao and her sister to wait for her. Gao insisted on going together with her, but Li Wa said, "No, I will ask my servant to accompany me. You'd better not look at the things that only pertain to women." Gao had to sit down and continue to drink tea.

After a while, the short maid came back alone with a letter in her hand, and Li Wa was not with her. Gao became anxious, and asked what happened at once. The servant said, "Just now a boy came here. He seemed to know Li Wa and gave her this letter. After reading this letter, she asked me to present it to you, and she got in the carriage and left."

Gao read the letter straightaway. This letter was written by a doctor in a hospital. It said that Li Wa's adoptive mother was dying of a serious illness, and asked Li Wa to meet her in the hospital immediately. Gao became irritated at once and shouted at Li Wa's sister, "At such a critical moment, how could she leave all by herself? Why didn't she go there with me?"

Her sister, who was sitting beside him, took the letter and read. She said, "How could Li Wa go away without telling us? Don't feel irritated. Li Wa must be so worried about our mother that she didn't know what to do. Now I will ask the maid to get a carriage for you, so you can find her in the hospital."

Feeling both irritated and anxious, Gao had no alternative but to wait for the carriage. After a long time, the carriage finally arrived at the gate. Gao rushed to the hospital mentioned in the letter. Upon his arrival, he was told that Li Wa and her mother had never come.

Gao suspected that the hospital's address was wrong, so he went to Li Wa's house by carriage. On the way, he thought, "They may have returned home, or Li Wa's adoptive mother may have died all of a sudden. They may have gone to a coffin shop, or headed for another hospital...."

The carriage reached Li Wa's house at dinner time. Entering the gate, Gao was too surprised to say anything. He found that all the rooms were dark and nobody was in. He shouted several times, but no one replied. He searched each room, and found even the furniture had vanished.

Gao didn't know what had happened, and was speechless for quite some time. He stood at the gate thinking about the past. He wouldn't believe Li Wa, who deeply loved him, would leave him in such a haste.

He wouldn't believe what had happened. He trusted Li Wa's love for him. She had been undoubtedly in love with him.

He must find her to discover the reason.

The carriage had left. He walked alone for a long time, and eventually got to the gate of the garden where he went in the afternoon. He was tired and angry, but he still knocked at the thick gate with great force. It was so late that people had gone for a rest, so no one would open the gate for him. He sat at the gate of the garden and began to cry. Being thirsty and hungry, he cried until he fell asleep.

The next morning he woke up. He knocked at the gate with great strength again. After a short while, an old servant opened the door and asked him what he wanted to do. He said, "I want to see Li Wa. No, I want to see Li Wa's sister. Is this her house?"

The old servant looked at him in a doubtful way and said, "Young man, you must get it wrong. This is the Zhang's garden. The Zhang family doesn't live in Chang'an, and there is no woman in the family other than a 90-year-old granny. I am the servant of this family and have been in charge of the garden for two decades. I have never heard of anyone called Li Wa or her sister." Gao didn't believe that and said, "It can't be true. I came to the garden yesterday afternoon. It was a short maidservant who opened the gate."

The old servant thought for a while and said, "Ah, I see. The Zhang family seldom comes to the garden, so they often rent it out. The day before yesterday, a short maidservant came to rent the garden. She told me that her master would like to stay here for two days. But they went away before dinner time yesterday. There is no one in the garden now. If you don't believe me, you can come and take a look." Gao searched every corner of the garden to no avail, and finally he sat at the table in the middle of the garden and began to cry.

After a while, Gao calmed down and was offered some tea by the old servant. Then he told the servant how he spent the past year and what happened yesterday.

Hearing this, the old servant looked at him and said, "Young man, you may have been deceived by the courtesan. Most of the young people like you must have taken a lot of money when they come to Chang'an for the imperial exam. They have no friends here, so some evil people would take advantage of them. It is so unfortunate that such a thing occurred to you. You'd better contact your parents as soon as possible and have them pick you up and send you home."

Better Die Than Live

Gao was filled with remorse. He had no place to go and no acquaintances. He felt so sorry for his parents and dared not return home. He was angry with Li Wa and her adoptive mother, but was even more so with himself. He wandered along and subconsciously walked to Li Wa's house. He sat on the ground in a daze without eating and drinking. He would rather die than live.

Hearing what had happened to him, all the neighbors felt sad for him and some of them offered him meals and allowed him to stay at the gate of their houses. At any rate, it was better to sleep there than on the roadside. Gao felt he was no better than a dog and was very upset.

Soon, Gao fell seriously ill and was on the verge of death.

His neighbors then sent him to the coffin shop. Although they sympathized with him, they had no means to help him.

The people in the coffin shop were kind to him. They offered him egg soup every day and hoped he would get better soon. After one month, he did recover and could stand up by himself. Gao had no place to go, so he decided to stay to lend them a hand. He worked here for three years.

Gao was good at calligraphy and also excelled in singing. This helped the shop owner a lot. In the Tang Dynasty, when people died, their family members would invite singers in the funeral home to eulogize the good deeds of the deceased.

Relatives and friends of the dead would be moved to tears by good singers, and would leave a lot of money to the funeral home. Thus good singers would become very popular and valuable.

In Chang'an, a singing contest was held every three years in the largest market so as to select the best singer among those in the funeral homes. Gao read a lot, so he was good at writing songs. His pieces were full of emotion and could easily move others. That year's singing competition was just around the corner. The owner of the coffin shop asked Gao to take part in the contest.

The contest lasted three days. Local people and visitors all came to listen to it. Among the listeners, there was an old acquaintance of Gao—an old servant from Changzhou who had worked in the Gao family for 30 years and had witnessed Gao's growth. In the distance, the old servant noticed a young man singing and could hardly believe his own eyes.

That young man was none other than Lord Gao Junior! But he

began to doubt himself. Why did he sing here? The old servant inquired about where the young man came from. He was told that the young man was from Changzhou. All his money was swindled by a courtesan, and he dared not return home to meet his parents, so he had to stay here.

The old servant thought that must be Gao and he must tell this to Lord Gao. But why is it that the old servant was in Chang'an? Well, he came to Chang'an with Lord Gao on business. When Lord Gao was engaged in his work, the servant would go out for a walk. Somehow he found himself at the big market.

The old servant scuttled back to the hotel where Lord Gao stayed. As he entered, he cried and told Lord Gao that he saw his son. Hearing what the servant said, Lord Gao was astonished and said, "What? Did you really see my son? Where is he?"

The old servant told him the singing contest in the market, the love between Li Wa and Gao…. Lord Gao wouldn't believe what the servant said. He said, "You must be wrong. My son is a good boy. He is fond of reading. How could he fall in love with a courtesan? After he took 3,000 taels of silver and left with his servants, I didn't get any news from him. I thought he must have been killed on his way. How could he sing songs for a funeral home? It must be another person who resembles my son."

With tears in his eyes, the old servant insisted on having Lord Gao go and see for himself. Lord Gao had no choice but to get on the carriage and reached the market with the old servant. It was afternoon now, and all the spectators were gone. Gao was cleaning the streets with several young people. The old servant came to Gao and clutched his clothes. Gao lifted his head and found that man was none other than the old servant of his family. He turned around and wanted to run away. But the old servant grabbed him and cried out in tears, "Where are you going? Your father is here! Where on earth are you going?"

Gao felt too ashamed to see his father, but he was moved by the old servant's tears. Finally, he was pulled by the servant to the carriage parked at a distance where Lord Gao sat and observed them.... Gao got in the carriage and felt fearful. He dared not look at his father while Lord Gao ignored him on purpose. Lord Gao said to the old servant, "Get out of the town." Then he kept silent.

When they went out of the town, Lord Gao asked his servant to wait beside the carriage, but he pulled his son out of the carriage and came to a vacant place. Without saying anything, he began to whip Gao until blood was all over his body. Lord Gao beat him while crying. In the end, his son couldn't move at all.

Lord Gao cried and said, "We've received no news since you left four years ago. Your mother and I thought you must have been killed on your way. We felt heart-broken. We had never expected that you would stay with a courtesan in Chang'an.... Why is it that our family bred a son of such bad conduct? I'll beat you to death today. I am no longer your father and you are not my son anymore." With these words, Lord Gao went away by himself.

Gao, who was bleeding and experiencing extreme pain, lay on the ground in a daze. How he hoped he were dead now! He felt sorry for his parents. He felt too shameful to survive. He no longer wanted to sing. He wanted to die in this way.

Met the Beauty Again

From that day on, Gao wandered around Chang'an and begged

for meals. He seemed to be dead although he was alive.

Winter approached soon. On a snowy morning, Gao was cold and hungry. He stood on the snow-covered ground to beg for meals. Then he walked to a lane and noticed a big gate of a courtyard was half open. Gao sat at the gate and cried out, "I am so hungry! I am so hungry! Please show mercy on me! Please offer me a meal!" His voice was miserable. Whoever heard the voice would burst into tears. Gao didn't know it was Li Wa who lived inside.

At the moment, Li Wa heard Gao's voice and was very amazed. She said to her servant, "This must be Gao. I recognized his voice!" With these words, she ran out immediately.

Gao was out of shape, extremely thin with little clothes on. At the sight of Li Wa, he fainted without saying a word. Li Wa stepped forward and held him in her arms, and asked her servant to help her bring Gao to her room. Li Wa let him lie on her bed and ordered her servant to bring hot soup for him.

While Li Wa was washing for Gao with warm water, she wept and said, "It is me who plunged you into today's situation!" Li Wa's mother heard the voice and ran into the room to see what had happened. At the sight of Gao, she ordered the servant, "Get the beggar out of here! Why did you allow him in?"

Li Wa said angrily to her mother, "No, he is from a decent family. He brought so much money to our family and spent it all in less than one year. If we send him away, he could neither return home nor have any other place to go. All our old neighbors know that I am the culprit. His parents have a lot of friends in Chang'an. Once they find out about what happened to him, they would get even with us. Can you get away with it then?"

After hearing this, the evil-minded adoptive mother became fearful. Li Wa focused her eyes on her and said, "I was sold to you ten years ago and have served as your daughter ever since. I've swindled tens of thousands of taels of silver for you. Now that you are 60 years old, I will give you another ten thousand taels of silver for your future life. I will leave you and live with Gao from now on. If you don't agree, I won't treat you as my mother anymore."

The old lady had no alternative but to accept the money and let her leave. Li Wa still had 1,000 taels of silver when she left. She thought, "I can live with Gao for quite some time with the money." She rented a small courtyard outside the town and lived with Gao in it. She cooked for him every day and invited doctors to cure his disease. After he became better several months later, Li Wa accompanied him to buy many books.

When he was fully recovered, Gao began to prepare for the imperial examination in the upcoming year with the encouragement of Li Wa. Apart from meals and sleep, he concentrated on learning. In the evening, Li Wa often sat beside Gao while he was studying.

The next year, Gao did come out first in the final imperial examination. The emperor dispatched him to serve as a local official in Chengdu. Before he left Chang'an, Li Wa said to him, "You've become the Number One Scholar that your parents wished you to be. I won't feel guilty for you anymore. It's time for me to leave. Although I love you deeply, we cannot get married because I used to be a courtesan but you are from a decent family and are appointed a local official now. You are supposed to marry a girl who comes from a wealthy family.

Now I have to come back to my mother's home since she is too old to live alone.

Gao wouldn't let her go in any case. He cried and said, "If you leave me, I will commit suicide immediately. I wouldn't survive without you...." Li Wa had no alternative but to agree to accompany him to Chengdu and leave by then.

Reunion

After more than 20 days on the journey to Chengdu, Gao and Li Wa came across the old servant of Lord Gao in a hotel. Why did this occur? His father happened to stay in this hotel on his way to deal with a business. They had no idea that they lived in the same hotel. What a coincidence!

Gao found his father and admitted his wrongdoings. Seeing his son was still alive, Lord Gao burst into tears. The two embraced each other and cried for a long time. Lord Gao and his son thus became reconciled. Lord Gao asked about his life over the past two years. His son told him what had happened as well as Li Wa's intended departure.

After hearing this, Lord Gao lowered his head and thought for a while, then said, "Without Li Wa's help, you wouldn't have had the chance of starting your life anew, let alone surviving to become the Number One Scholar, and the Gao family would have lost you forever. I will arrange everything for you."

The next morning, Lord Gao arranged a carriage to send Gao to Chengdu. On the third day, he asked Li Wa to live in a courtyard which his servant was ordered to rent. On the fourth day, Lord Gao brought up a proposal of marriage to Li Wa and planned to have Li Wa marry his son.

Li Wa was moved to tears because she had never imagined that Lord Gao would allow them to get married. Li Wa was a good wife as well as a good daughter-in-law. She treated her in-laws very well, and her in-laws liked her very much. From then on, the Gao family lived a happy life. The young couple then gave birth to four sons, who also lived happily later.

Although many years have passed, seniors in Chang'an continue to tell their youth the story of Li Wa, the story about selflessness and audacity to love.

练习题 Reading exercises

一、选择题。Choose the correct answers.

1. 高老爷是高公子的什么人？（　　）

   A. 爸爸　　B. 老师　　C. 老仆人　　D. 哥哥

2. 李娃住在哪里？（　　）

   A. 常州　　B. 长安　　C. 北京　　D. 杭州

3. 高公子第一次出远门是去哪里？（　　）

   A. 常州　　B. 成都　　C. 北京　　D. 长安

4. 谁和高公子一起去了长安？（　　）

   A. 高老爷　　B. 老师　　C. 侍女　　D. 两个仆人

5. 高公子到长安去做什么？（　　）

   A. 去结婚　　B. 去看病　　C. 去考试　　D. 去旅游

6. 高公子第一次去李娃家带了多少两银子？（　　）

   A. 300　　B. 150　　C. 100　　D. 3000

7. 高老爷有几个儿子？（　　）

   A. 一个　　B. 两个　　C. 三个　　D. 没有

8. 高公子去长安的时候，高老爷给他带了多少两银子？（　　）

   A. 150　　B. 100　　C. 500　　D. 3000

9. 高公子在李娃家住了多久以后，就没钱了？（　　）

　　A. 三天　　B. 一个月　　C. 一年　　D. 两年

10. 当高公子没有钱再给李娃的养母的时候，他先卖掉了车和马，然后又卖掉了什么？（　　）

　　A. 书　　B. 仆人　　C. 衣服　　D. 房子

11. 为什么李娃的养母对高公子越来越不好？（　　）

　　A. 因为养母心情不好

　　B. 因为养母生病了

　　C. 因为养母看高公子没钱了

　　D. 因为养母觉得高公子没礼貌

12. 李娃对高公子说想去郊区玩儿几天，是什么意思？（　　）

　　A. 李娃不想待在城里　　B. 李娃想去郊区生活
　　C. 李娃想离开养母　　D. 李娃想离开高公子

13. 邻居们为什么同情高公子？（　　）

　　A. 因为高公子很可怜　　B. 因为高公子很好看
　　C. 因为高公子很有钱　　D. 因为高公子读书很好

14. 李娃离开高公子以后，高公子为什么不回家？（　　）

　　A. 他没脸回家见父母　　B. 他还想找到李娃
　　C. 他没钱回家　　D. 他喜欢住在长安

15. 李娃留下高公子,自己一个人从花园门口坐车走了,理由是什么?(　　)

　　A. 她要去买东西　　　B. 她家里着火了

　　C. 她的养母生病了　　D. 她的养母死了

16. 高老爷和老仆人到长安来是为了(　　)。

　　A. 工作的事　　B. 找儿子　　C. 买东西　　D. 旅游

17. 高公子家的老仆人在哪里看到了高公子?(　　)

　　A. 花园里　　B. 大市场　　C. 大路上　　D. 医馆里

18. 老仆人不敢相信自己的眼睛,因为他看见高公子在干什么?(　　)

　　A. 读书　　B. 要饭　　C. 吃饭　　D. 唱歌

19. 李娃为了能和高公子一起生活,给了养母多少两银子?(　　)

　　A. 1000　　B. 10000　　C. 3000　　D. 150

20. 高公子和李娃结婚后生了几个孩子?(　　)

　　A. 一个　　B. 四个　　C. 两个　　D. 三个

二、判断题：请根据故事内容判断下列说法是否正确，如果正确请标"T"，不正确请标"F"。
Decide whether the following statements are true (T) or false (F).

1. 高公子19岁的时候，第一次离开家去长安。（   ）
2. 高老爷给高公子带了2000两银子。（   ）
3. 高公子到长安后，只看了几天书就再也不想看了。（   ）
4. 高公子第一次看到李娃的时候，觉得她不好看。（   ）
5. 李娃的养母看到高公子带来的银子很生气。（   ）
6. 高公子住在李娃家，他的仆人很高兴。（   ）
7. 高公子的仆人希望高公子好好读书。（   ）
8. 一天，高公子和李娃说想去郊外玩儿。（   ）
9. 高公子住在李娃家的一年里，李娃的养母越来越喜欢高公子。（   ）
10. 高老爷在长安看到自己的儿子还活着，非常开心。（   ）
11. 高老爷一点儿也不生儿子的气，马上带他离开长安，回家了。（   ）
12. 李娃看到要饭的高公子，难过地哭了。（   ）
13. 高老爷最终原谅了儿子。（   ）
14. 高老爷不同意高公子和李娃结婚。（   ）
15. 结婚后，李娃对高公子的父母非常好。（   ）

三、选择填空。Choose the appropriate words to fill in the blanks.

1. 高公子是高老爷的儿子，高老爷只有这一个_____。高公子非常_____，读书很_____，在学校考试的成绩总是第一名。高老爷为自己的儿子感到很_____。这一年，皇帝在全国招考状元，高老爷决定让儿子去长安参加_____。常州到长安的路很远，高公子_____走了一个月，终于走到了长安。在他的眼里，长安到处都是_____的东西。

    A. 好玩儿   B. 聪明   C. 考试   D. 孩子
    E. 用心   F. 大约   G. 骄傲

2. 高公子一开始还看了几天书，_____一个月后，他就_____也不想读书了。原来，他觉得别人的想法都_____他，他心里有些_____了。他决定先不看书了，还是每天出去_____吧。从那以后，他每天都骑马出门，_____看看_____看看，_____逛到天都黑了才回宾馆。

    A. 总要   B. 可是   C. 不如   D. 逛逛
    E. 再   F. 得意   G. 东   H. 西

3. 李娃长得太漂亮了，这样_____的姑娘，高公子从来都没见过。为了能和李娃在一起，高公子第二天就拿了300两银子来到李娃家。李娃的养母告诉高公子，李娃喜欢_____跳舞，也喜欢和他这样的年轻人_____。和李娃在一起，高公子觉得太_____了。就这样，他们两个人一直_____到了吃晚饭的时候。

A. 唱歌　　B. 好看　　C. 交朋友　　D. 聊

E. 幸福

4. 第二年考试的时候，高公子_____中了状元。皇帝派他去成都做地方官。高公子要离开长安的时候，李娃对他说："_____你终于像你父母希望的那样成了状元，我已经对得起你了。我该走了。_____很爱你，可是我以前是妓女，你是好人家的儿子，现在又是地方官，我们_____结婚。你_____找一个有钱的大小姐结婚。"

A. 不能　　B. 虽然　　C. 现在　　D. 真的

E. 应该

四、连线题。 Match.

1. 请为下列人物和地点连线。

   A. 李娃　　　　　a. 长安

   B. 高老爷　　　　b. 常州

   C. 养母

2. 根据故事内容为下列人物选择各自的特征。

   A. 李娃　　　　　a. 聪明的

   B. 高公子　　　　b. 好看的

   C. 老仆人　　　　c. 坏心的

   D. 养母　　　　　d. 善良的

3. 根据故事内容为下列人物选择各自的身份。

   A. 高公子　　　　a. 长安的妓女

   B. 李娃　　　　　b. 高老爷的儿子

   C. 高老爷　　　　c. 常州的大官

五、请根据故事内容给下列句子排列顺序。
Put the following statements in order according to the story.

1.

A. 李娃的养母听见李娃房间里有声音,就跑过来看发生了什么事。

B. 坏心的养母一听这话害怕了。

C. 李娃非常生气地对养母说:"不行!他是好人家的儿子。当年带着那么多钱来到我家,不到一年,钱就花光了。我们想办法赶走了他,他不能回家,也没有地方去。我们以前的邻居都知道他是因为我李娃才变成这样的。他的父亲母亲家有很多朋友在长安。如果有一天他们知道了高公子的事,要来找我们,那时候你跑得了吗?"

D. 一看是高公子,她马上对侍女说:"快把这个要饭的赶走!为什么要让他进门?"

E. 李娃一边用热水给高公子洗身体,一边哭着说:"你变成今天这样,都是因为我啊!"

2.

A. 有几个好心的邻居还拿来饭菜给他吃。

B. 被李娃抛弃的高公子后悔极了。

C. 他就这么呆呆地坐在李娃家门口的地上,不吃不喝,觉得自己生不如死。

D. 邻居们听说了他的事，都很同情他。

E. 他觉得自己对不起父母，没有脸回家。他对李娃母女很生气，但他更生自己的气。

F. 他走啊走啊，不知什么时候又走到了李娃家门口。

六、图片题。 Answer the following questions according to the pictures.

1. 请根据你的记忆，说说下面这幅图所画的故事情节。

2. 下面这幅图中,和高公子说话的人物是谁?

3. 下面这幅图中,李娃在做什么?

4. 下面这幅图中，高公子的心情怎么样？

5. 请你用中文或英文给下面这幅图加一个简单的标题。

七、思考题。 Answer the questions according to the story.

1. 李娃是一个怎样的女人？请说一说你的看法。

2. 高老爷爱自己的儿子吗？请说一说你的看法。

部分练习题答案 Keys to the exercises

一、选择题
1. A   2. B   3. D   4. D   5. C
6. A   7. A   8. D   9. C   10. B
11. C   12. D   13. A   14. A   15. C
16. A   17. B   18. D   19. B   20. B

二、判断题：请根据故事内容判断下列说法是否正确，如果正确请标"T"，不正确请标"F"
1. T   2. F   3. T   4. F   5. F
6. F   7. T   8. F   9. F   10. F
11. F   12. T   13. T   14. F   15. T

三、选择填空
1. D B E G C F A
2. B E C F D G H A
3. B A C E D
4. D C B A E

四、连线题
1. A-a, B-b, C-a   2. A-b, B-a, C-d, D-c
3. A-b, B-a, C-c

五、请根据故事内容给下列句子排列顺序
1. E-A-D-C-B   2. B-E-F-C-D-A

词汇表
Vocabulary List

鞭子	n.	biānzi	whip
宾馆	n.	bīnguǎn	hotel
不幸	adj.	búxìng	unfortunate
长	v.	zhǎng	grow
成都	n.	Chéngdū	Chengdu, capital city of Sichuan Province
重新	adv.	chóngxīn	anew, again
床	n.	chuáng	bed
大官	n.	dà guān	high-ranking official
呆	adv.	dāi	in a daze
当地	n.	dāngdì	locality
儿媳	n.	érxí	daughter-in-law
封	m.w.	fēng	(for sth. enveloped)
干涉	v.	gānshèn	meddle, intervene
赶紧	adv.	gǎnjǐn	hurriedly, without delay
棺材铺	n.	guāncaipù	coffin shop
和好	v.	héhǎo	become reconciled
后悔	v.	hòuhuǐ	regret, be remorseful
花园	n.	huāyuán	garden
皇帝	n.	Huángdì	emperor
回	v.	huí	return
回报	v.	huíbào	reward
浑身	n.	húnshēn	all over the body
急	adj.	jí	irritated, anxious
妓女	n.	jìnǚ	courtesan
接	v.	jiē	pick up
举起	v.	jǔqǐ	lift, raise
举行	v.	jǔxíng	hold, host
开心	adj.	kāixīn	happy
可怜	v.	kělián	have pity on, show mercy on

老板	n.	lǎobǎn	shop owner
老太太	n.	lǎotàitai	old lady
连忙	adv.	liánmáng	immediately
两	m.w.	liǎng	*liang* (a unit of weight, equal to 50 grams)
流泪	v.	liú lèi	weep
母女	n.	mǔnǚ	mother and daughter
难过	adj.	nánguò	sad, sorrowful
您	pron.	nín	you, a polite form of 你
派	v.	pài	send, dispatch
骗	v.	piàn	deceive
品行	n.	pǐnxíng	moral conduct
仆人	n.	púrén	servant
骑	v.	qí	ride
敲	v.	qiāo	knock
去世	v.	qùshì	pass away
人生	n.	rénshēng	life
市场	n.	shìchǎng	market
侍女	n.	shìnǚ	maidservant
瘦	adj.	shòu	thin
态度	n.	tàidù	manner, bearing
汤	n.	tāng	soup
唐朝	n.	Tángcháo	Tang Dynasty (618—907)
躺	v.	tǎng	lie
提亲	v.	tíqīn	bring up a proposal of marriage on behalf of a boy's or girl's family
同情	v.	tóngqíng	sympathize
团圆	v.	tuányuán	have a reunion
消息	n.	xiāoxi	news
心软	adj.	xīnruǎn	tender-hearted
醒	v.	xǐng	wake up
血	n.	xiě	blood
养母	n.	yǎngmǔ	adoptive mother
养女	n.	yǎngnǚ	adoptive daughter
医馆	n.	yīguǎn	hospital (in ancient times)
以后	n.	yǐhòu	later

以前	n.	yǐqián	before
银子	n.	yínzi	silver
勇敢	adj.	yǒnggǎn	brave, audacious
游逛	v.	yóuguàng	stroll about, wander
于是	conj.	yúshì	then
院子	n.	yuànzi	courtyard
晕	adj.	yūn	dizzy, fainted
招考	v.	zhāokǎo	recruit through examination
主意	n.	zhǔyi	idea
转身	v.	zhuǎnshēn	turn around
状元	n.	Zhuàngyuan	Number One Scholar in a nationwide imperial examination
自从	prep.	zìcóng	from, since
自信	adj.	zìxìn	confident
租	v.	zū	rent

项目策划：韩　颖　刘小琳
责任编辑：韩　颖
英文翻译：吴爱俊
英文编辑：薛彧威
英文审订：黄长奇
封面设计：E·T创意工作室

图书在版编目（CIP）数据

李娃传：汉、英／侯琨改编．— 北京：华语教学出版社，2016
（"彩虹桥"汉语分级读物．3级：750词）
ISBN 978-7-5138-1102-6

Ⅰ．①李… Ⅱ．①侯… Ⅲ．①汉语－对外汉语教学－语言读物 Ⅳ．① H195.5

中国版本图书馆 CIP 数据核字（2015）第 308003 号

李娃传

侯　琨　改编

*

©华语教学出版社有限责任公司
华语教学出版社有限责任公司出版
（中国北京百万庄大街24号　邮政编码 100037）
电话：(86)10-68320585　68997826
传真：(86)10-68997826　68326333
网址：www.sinolingua.com.cn
电子信箱：hyjx@sinolingua.com.cn
新浪微博地址：http://weibo.com/sinolinguavip
北京京华虎彩印刷有限公司印刷
2016年（32开）第1版
2016年第1版第1次印刷
（汉英）
ISBN 978-7-5138-1102-6
定价：19.00元